D1709556

ANIMAL FAMILIES / FAMILIAS DE ANIMALES

LIONS / LEONES
LIFE IN THE PRIDE / VIDA EN LA MANADA

Willow Clark Traducción al español: Eduardo Alamán

PowerKiDS
press.
New York

Published in 2011 by The Rosen Publishing Group, Inc.
29 East 21st Street, New York, NY 10010

First Edition

Editor: Jennifer Way   Traducción al español: Eduardo Alamán
Book Design: Julio Gil

Photo Credits: Cover, pp. 9, 24 (top left) Digital Vision/Thinkstock; back cover © www.iStockphoto.com/ vectorcartoons; pp. 4–5, 21, 23, 24 (bottom right) Anup Shah/Photodisc/Thinkstock; pp. 7 (main), 11, 15, 17 (inset top, inset bottom), 24 (top middle, bottom left) iStockphoto/Thinkstock; p. 7 (inset) Hemera/ Thinkstock; p. 12–13 Tom Brakefield/Stockbyte/Thinkstock; p. 16–17 (main) Stockbyte/Thinkstock; p. 19 Anup Shah/Digital Vision/Thinkstock; p. 24 (top right) Jupiterimages/Photos.com/Thinkstock.

Library of Congress Cataloging-in-Publication Data
Clark, Willow.
 [Lions. Spanish & English]
 Lions = Leones : life in the pride : vida en la manada / by Willow Clark. — 1st ed.
    p. cm. — (Animal families = Familias de animales)
 Includes index.
 ISBN 978-1-4488-3140-1 (library binding)
 1. Lion—Juvenile literature. 2. Familial behavior in animals—Juvenile literature. I. Title. II. Title: Leones.
 QL737.C23C532418 2011
 599.757—dc22
                                    2010025996

Manufactured in the United States of America

CPSIA Compliance Information: Batch #WW11PK: For Further Information contact Rosen Publishing, New York, New York at 1-800-237-9932

Web Sites: Due to the changing nature of Internet links, PowerKids Press has developed an online list of Web sites related to the subject of this book. This site is updated regularly. Please use this link to access the list: www.powerkidslinks.com/afam/lions/

CONTENTS

CONTENIDO

Lions live together in a group, called a **pride**.

Los leones viven en grupos llamados **manadas**.

Lions live in **grasslands** in Africa.

Los leones viven en las **praderas** de África.

Africa
—
África

The pride raises its young together. Young lions are called **cubs**.

Las manadas crian a los pequeños leones en grupo. Estos pequeños leones se llaman **cachorros**.

Male lions have **manes**. They also roar loudly.

Los leones macho tienen **melenas**. Además, rugen muy fuerte.

Mane
Melena

Female lions are lionesses.
Mothers, daughters, and sisters
belong to the same pride.

Las hembras se llaman leonas
Las madres, hijas y hermanas
pertenecen a la misma manada.

Female cubs stay with their prides. Male cubs join new groups of lionesses.

Los cachorros hembra se quedan en la manada. Los cachorros macho se unen a otros grupos de leonas.

14

Lionesses do most of the hunting for the pride. They hunt zebras and wildebeests.

Las leonas se encargan de cazar. Las leonas cazan cebras y ñus.

Zebra
Cebra

Wildebeest
Ñu

17

The male lions watch the cubs while the lionesses hunt for the pride's food.

Mientras las leonas salen de cacería, los machos cuidan a los cachorros.

The lionesses bring food back to the pride. The males eat first. The cubs eat last.

Las leonas llevan comida a la manada. Los machos comen primero. Los cachorros comen al final.

Lions rest most of the day. While resting, they sleep, play, and **groom** each other.

Los leones descansan la mayor parte del día. Al descansar, duermen, juegan y se **limpian** unos a otros.

Words to Know / Palabras que debes saber

cubs / (los) cachorros

grasslands / (las) praderas

groom / limpiar

mane / (la) melena

pride / (la) manada